She Bang Slam

Erik Wackernagel

She Bang Slam

Erik Wackernagel

InExile Publications
Quebec

National Library of Canada Cataloguing in Publication
Wackernagel, Erik, 1988-

She Bang Slam / Erik Wackernagel
Poetry.

Includes bibliographical references.
ISBN 978-0-9876759-0-3
1. Poetry, Slam Poetry, American Literature.

InExile Publications
Sherbrooke, Quebec, Canada.
Typesetting & Cover Design: InExile Design

Cover Illustrations: Salvadore Dali, Raphaelesque Head Expoding, 1951.
Private Collection. Image release from © Demart Pro Arte B.V./DACs,
London, 1990.

CONTENTS

Paper my hide

If you think I write well,
It is because the paper is worn over
with clumps of my skin
puckering clutches of hair
holding on
with some biomechanical will.
Deer rolling under the bumper
of an '80 Camaro apple-wax red
write exquisite verse –
The best lines are cached
On the inside of the skin.
They come out only when you cut,
holding on to interior pores.
We're all in line for the Autopsy
Double-Feature at the drive-in
in 1955
where I left my favorite pen.

———————————

Living as a Poet

Put your hands up clicks the voice of thumb on hammer
in the side pocket running down from the fourth stanza,
As couplets leak down gutters and spill their
lives on the sidewalk.
The register clicks open swing clack on the sound of quarters
as bills pile up on the pavement with metal clips drop down hinges
on the face of Washington
Monument throwing the bird to the sky at the power of words.

Rustling cars in the hustle,
Throwback cowboys flushing down the wind tunnel of time.
Stealing horses frontal from the saloon slick with the stream
Rushing slack from the monsoon as the sky opens
and slashes nine holes in gashes across the face of Arizona.
The poet hits 18 holes in 18 strikes and strikes down golf carts,
Twisting triple aluminum axles off cliffsides
while the grass burns up in the night.
Light flooding flares as flames take off on the runway
in fallen forest blasphemy of trees cropped like dusters,
Flying passes over the powerlines and shooting the zits off
the faces of snickers-crazed teenagers.

Running a thin rail on credit and caffeine,
The poet packs heat as street lights shoot down
Little stories for kids who listen on 120 volt wires.
Surging over the newswire as NATO shoots down planes in Libya,
I am a journalist and a liar.
Walk the street I keep eyes in my hands words in my wallet –
Cards stack sharp in the tabs and cut the party membership lard.

Mustang runs rubber slicks like slabs hot on the asphalt,
Motor whistling theft and what is left falls to the wayside.
Banks flow empty promises in mouth salaried sockets clicking
Teeth while vaults empty in pockets and suits shimmy up bodies,
Smooth as a blowjob.

And a masked voice says empty it buster
through mad eyes.
Cashier says I play this game sometimes with my boyfriend –
You want to go in the safe right?

Jack of all Maids gets laid on the bar table and
Wide eyed screams in the lightbulb of trickery,
When coyotes pace around bony toes tingling in boots.

7-11 butters up Pepsi packs in the store window.
Rolls of chrome saunter by on Cadillacs
and rolled up dollar bills for the taking
Shoot out of 12-gauge shells loaded under the counter
while ribbed barrels fly into ribbed condoms
in the death fetish closet.

We spring with words on hollow legs from rooftops,
Watching the marvels circulate at the level of ants,
Watching marbles roll downstream with our intelligence in hand.
Poetry taints the architectural designs of human spiders with decay.
Walls fracture from the pressure penetrated by rhyme.
Cash may be forthcoming in the tumor light of commercials,
but sometimes we die cold at the bottom of staircases
Blanketed only by the dark of deafness,
as skyscrapers seek not to hear the words saturating the sheetrock.
And suicide resonates like crystal glasses of wine in the walls,
And civilization rolls past our eyes like tumbleweed in a Western
Or in the heart of the forest the trees creak in humidity
to escape their bodies and speak through silent root connections
Fibers draped in buried streams shooting words on the wire of water
as poetry predates language
Stretch limbs to leap in cartoon fragments as the lyric flings
Skin to the air and we seek to supersede the human body,

. . .

Warriors swooping midnight archery sliding down the Milky Way.
Words and flaming arrows dot the sky
As one by one
We empty out our cash pockets to poetry
and militant rhythms ring down bells of the hour
until conflict means love.

Untitled in Red

Autumn comes quick as the birds shed their fetters.
We write letters with the fervor of leaves cracking
The string that holds them to their fathers.
Only in death can we be individuals, they say.
Floating onto a breeze gentle but cold,
Yet they do not make it much farther than the apples.
Life on their own may mean brittle fractures
Under the spectrum of possible footfalls.
The urge to speak burns up its last reservoirs
Of intensity. Vocal cords striking whips
Against the retreating sun.
Tongues cry against those we wish
Would come back to us.
Shuddering wings give hale to the nest
And some of them head off to dark coasts in Guyana
While dark masters ring the sky in masses,
Cawing to the rhythm of dirges sung by
Deer knocked down dark stairs on the roadway.
The early bird gets the worm, and the late bird
Gets the leftovers, and mocks the shaky hands
Of apes retreating into the cave.
Far-off comrades blink in mental pictures
Stained with tears, blotted with ink running
Black lifelines down worn pages. We will
Not be wanting for time to write of adventures
Lost across the sweeping wing of the Milky Way,
While latent thoughts sit freezing slowly
In ears turning red at the elfish tips.
Brittle as frosty pine needles drooping
In the direction of powder.

. . .

Before the fire paints its loud grin
On coal-stained glass faces, lava heat
Seeping transparent in black iron bodies –
The ravens let out the last cackle,
Faster than two-stroke motors.
Hands rough and thick from
A sort of photosynthesis,
Pulling the dirty cord for the last times.
Pulling the plug to watch ink-drawn correspondences
Drain through the gleaming artifice –
Pipes running through the intestines of the world,
So our words may pop up in the ass
Of old friends out from under the ocean.
Letters tinged in red from the cool breath
Of the sun's retreat,
I hear the dry wings flapping
From far-off through the window.

Let it come quick.
Birds do not wait, and neither do words.

Staple my Skin

Staple my skin,
I am nothing but words and nerves
Strung up a spine knit by trembling hands,
Hung loose as a rope bridge,
Notched with shaky slats.
Try and cross me,
I refuse to fall without
Dropping human flies in the lake –
Lay your eggs fast.

Staple my skin,
The moment is past for conversation.
Digression drags patience in a choke,
Collar kissing the spinal cord,
Hoarding emotional motor responses
In crannies crawling up between vertebrae.
Nothing to say but the hum
Of tension soaking between syllables.
Sound drops like clear liquid
Down my back.
Words come out like scat,
The blackface little-known stories of jazz –
Better than coming back up.
Words sting in bile broth
Coming back up the throat after we swallow them.

Sew me up like a cheap hospital sheet,
Bleachy clean is a classy fate.
Mortality lies in dirt at both ends –
Skin is thicker than cotton.
Stretching lies in quiet fibers,
I grow silent as my mouth spits red.

. . .

Stitches and my tongue sheds its winter skin
Lying in the sweat falling off maples.
This summer everything get sealed up.
Staple cuts the shaky reflex.

Tranquility is a civil manner
By which to mangle the human body.
Quiet settles on tweed suits that used to itch,
Sipping red wine stems pinched in steady fingers
Until my sealed body explodes cherry stuffing
And thick noodles all over the banquet tables.

Gallery of the Silent Circus

Take this gallery:
Blood spattered walls,
The wheeling of patients
In wide gaping halls,
The canines of beauty
Massaging our skin;
Ever the risk of a puncture
Through the thin membrane
Of aesthetics.

Hook them up to your theory machines,
Pump them full of magazines,
Casings loaded with scenes of grotesque lives
All mired in the grain,
Loaded with severed members
And portraits of the sane.

What is this place you've brought us
on the precipice of a scream?
Where the turgid voices of balls and bearings
Subdivide our hearing,
And anonymous kidneys from Madagascar
Propped up in sterilized glass cases
Are driven around in black limousines
And nowhere
To be
Seen.

And who sits upon the torrid throne
Adorned in copper shells and leather:
The president of the United States

. . .

In someone's sallied underwear?
But is she really President
With the head of a wild boar,
Or simply the queen of diamonds
writhing on the floor?

And on to the puppet theater
To discover our inner children,
Starving and obese upon
The fodder that we feed 'em.
And watch the ghosts dance in the lights
On the whim of the wholly frothier,
Foaming in torturous orgasm
At our finest and most dispensable
Tumbling into the chasm.
For is it all but a stellar jazz performance
Or an injection of rectoplasm?

And when the staff of godliness
Goes to the highest bidder:
Will we all be forced to wash our selves
in troughs of kitty litter?
And bow our heads when standing
In the light of the projectionist,
And sing the giddy anthem
Of the horsemen of dissection.

The streets are ready for Christmas
With our regurgitated love.
The snow is mixed with blood and salt,
Our souls are frozen in the mud,
But this modern art is so beautiful
When it's stepping on your face,

So drink the puddles wet with souls
And swallow it with grace.

And wheel us around on the brim of lives
Forgotten in their own movements,
And lay me down old shepherd
In the warmth of my ever-blinking ward,
Please lay your hands upon me,
And let there be no more.

For is it all but a lie?
Festooned in scenes of
Beauty love and circuits,
Painted pieces on the stage
In the gallery of silent circus?
Or is it all just a flake of cardboard
Blowing through the alleys,
Flapping its squared off wings
In the year of the lord
our lord.

Nouveau Krystallnacht

And the players take the ready stage but where is the conductor,
by the moon's limelight of a glassy eye – the candy man he fucked her.

Nouveau Chic clad in steely limbs and AK-47s
Straw man and silky worm sprawled out by the 7-11
On the phone jingle jangle Santa Claus is coming home
1-800 Star 69 which way to the thunder dome?
Pick a battle on the ground choose your own endeavor
The smartest rat to smoke a pack can point the way to heaven

click clack on the mean streets
carbon monoxide athletes
the pounding heart of lead feet
crushing the crunch of fallen sleet

Pitter patter sings the sanguine symphony of sharding sand drops
The window frame sings an elegy to the step of the beat cops
And chain gangs fucking splinter coils of snowy glass around
On the night of the crystal whitey Christmas who can hear a sound

Beaming bright-eyed tragedies on the wave of hulking metal giants
Pearly faces on the nightly crystal screen are lying
But how to fly above the glassy music our horizon
And when the bouncing candy drops become too sweet a geyser

The tingle shatters on the eve of the saint who's trickin' us
Little by little piece by piece a mirror turns to dust
And the snow falls on a crystal tree that's not to be discussed

And the boots pound on
And the boots pound on
And they march into the night
Forever seduced by the stabbing song
Of the crystal gouging out our sight
And we listen and pray and live and dream on the whim of a teeter totter

And the pounding glass it plays its merry symphony ever louder
And the truth in the reflection is shattering on the ground
The truth is in the seven years of bad luck that we found
So march the march of happy hollow onward to the dawn
By train and bus and SS SOS onward till we're gone
And the song plays on
And the song plays on
Ever through the night
And the song plays on
And the song plays on
And every note is right

and the song plays on
and the song plays on
ever through the night
and the song pounds on
and the song pounds on
and every note is right

———————————

Red Specter Kill

We have placed the luminous spectrum under house arrest,
Fearing the risk of wildcat paw bats
On the part of colors, autonomous agents
Infecting the quickest port of entry to the human mind.
Once colors are moving, they blow through
Reticent windows like crumbling old napkins
Popping paparazzi shots in mirrors
That we had forgotten.

There is no catching a beast
Who slingshots itself riding airy cheetahs with
Six-packs of M-80's for feet.
Sexless, there is no fooling it with the
Mimicking tongues of orchids,
Much as we might like to see wild mating
Forces colliding at the speed of light.
Colors are a breed hard to tease.
They laugh at the ease
with which clumsy fingers catch rodents.

The momentary leap through the solar system
Does not make me cringe,
As the crimson of lips expelling tingles
Despite the closing of eyelids.
Sparks tickling the orange glands in Floridian taste buds
Quickly sketch the allure of carbon
Clinging to metal-skinned potatoes,

Yet they can't explain why
The human fires clutching to the bounds of imagination,
Strange in time and home,
Are white, and why the sun draws goosebumps
To arms seeking liberty in July.

The film will continue, despite the arresting
Silence of colors.

Gradient senses forget their old velocity;
Limbs settle thirsty in antebellum poses.
Faces are not sought for their expressionism
In the graphic science of terror. Strangely,
Blood is a poor mockup for blood in the moving lens.
Beets crack the dry western earth in
Ghastly whims to clutch white blouses that collect
The sparse and quivering residue of the color wheel.

The rainbow shrinks from the pressure hose
Spraying the Kindergarten. Abstaining words
Shut up the gathering climax speed of skeletal
Queers collecting in the water ducts,
Populating the paving stone landscape, haunting
Pumpkin-eyed families.
Color-eating goggles lie in shadowy patience
In birthing clinics.

The Theater of Cruelty, born in white halls,
Sniffing bleach and tactile blackouts,
Offers murmurs to a tonsilly collection plate,
Where pupils leak into homeless death orgies.
New doctors gently peel away light wave receptors,
Nails plucking cheese wax.

The curtains kiss with the first tap of cold light.
Infants incubate by the dozen in the cinema;
Seats menstruate old strips of velvet robbed of blush.
Hue-drained thighs stretch and lift off from the resting place.
Stand and applaud. The whites of their eyes meet
and embrace in quiet abandon. In padded walls
Stained only with the off-gassing of odd dreams –
Together we have seen the solution.

. . .

The exit lights flashing
Cast the pale glow of 1939
On summery flesh filing in the doorway.
The narrator chooses to remain anonymous.

For the Critics

These stories are blood spilling
On dry sheep skins with drops of salt –
Alphabets dry up and the stink of injury fades.
Hard to imagine scrawny hands clinging to records
Of one sick hand tracing the yellowy-red juice
Around on pages peeled from the Book of Death.
How many have mingled their blood on this page
Before my bones landed here?
Did some dilute it with piss to make watercolors?
Will the sun suck my scratches away
Or turn them black and hard?
Dense like the wood that bled pulp
To sustain history.

Hard to imagine bones snapping reflexive jaws
Against each other in dry bowls scattered
With stones and gummy roots,
Groping these bloody rambles
Like spilling cuts – Words seem thick and graphic
When fresh, but fade to a thin fluid.
Will time not cut the deadly will of fighting wrists
As it cuts the color of my voice?

Diffusing in weak pissy breezes,
Paper edges curling in dry bile floating in time,
Dust peppering the sky of vague settings,
Skin must be erased of its own markings
To be disgraced with words in foreign blood –
Toothless tongue lolling with flames
To fling nauseous thoughts on the scroll.

. . .

Flecks of excess raining on rocks ballooning with heat,
Aging is fast in this place.
Atmospheric eyes seem absent or laughing.
The sage fled with full lips,
Forsaking the game of blood forming and dripping
For the enrichment of future bones,
Cracking in locks, crumbled to soak up red water.
Nimble legs seeking flush red lips guarding
Forests blooming young on the roll call of centuries,
Cells rigid without words.
The flash of vines, on reverse lightning shots to the canopy,
Want nothing of documenting senescence.

All of this when I close my eyes,
Fingers locked onto mutton skins,
Growing dryer by the second.

Walking Bordello Map

There is a fuck leaning crass in the hollow door frame,
Smoke climbing the moldings nearly invisible.
Take a drag off the pipe of eyes running desperate into night uppers.

There is luck trapped in a corroded penny charmed leaning on the
sewer grate,
Daring us to let it fall washing away in piss with dead cats,
Blasting a grenade hole in the material world and crawling out.
There is an ambush lying in the roadside ditch.
Imperialist pawns live in constant fear terror is not a tactic
But a mechanism hinging on liquid pressure in the mind.

There is an ambush lurking in the console.
Ghostly hands rise out of the toggle,
Personnel petrified in eons flushed through in a second.

There are holes in our perception opening into
Apartment houses caught in a fog of graffiti and stalled time.
All it takes is a tiny opening a hole-punch can split the fibers
Of paper into a gaping crack in reality.
Syntax cuts bound in papers punched and lying in folders,
Stapled piling up on desks words seeking to illuminate
Often misguided piling up intellectual compost.

There is a syntax in the grid of sensations written on
The 1:1 map of streets emotions clouded in dust torn up by
Mustangs budding in the early spring spoilers can dub us whores.
There are curses deep in the throat of cheap hotels,
Slowly weaving patterns on ceilings owned by spiders
Sometimes they are cast in the base of chandeliers
Stuck on tonsils over predatory tongues.

. . .

There is time fracturing constant motion is stagnant
Hopping on hare legs frozen in photographs never taken.

There is a time to cut the inertia of minutes hopping unseen
Carrying people on 14-day Europe tours on a single street.
Can't always be kidnapped by the flushing mechanic.
Will can push hands to strike at pressure points in days
That cycle thoughtless on auxiliary power narrative momentum
Cuts up and collages the laws of Newton.
Particle colliders operate covertly in social networks.
Tension disappears and appears like electrons.
We speak like quanta at a distance.

Hard to capture the chemical structure of lies walking on two feet
With tired eyes when the sun is setting,
Letting away wispy hints of blue sky.
There is a cauldron brewing subtle inputs on a gas fire –
It keeps on cooking when the building drops.
There are flies dropping chronic in a wake around curses.

There are dreams sewing liquid suggestions into blueprints,
Mingling with coffee stains water drips from the ceiling.
There is a process of decomposition beginning in the senses,
Into the census surveying the holes of perception groaning cracks
In feet that walk on streets revolving three hundred and sixty degrees.

Three hundred sixty five days stepping unforgiving on dreams
Captured in photogenic plates glass sewn into the concrete.
Fracture to off-gas the words that tell us to stay –
There is a fuck in the doorway.

The rules of the game spoken in shadows looking into the building.
Who speaks but a straw-man standing up on on splinters

From doors broken in under particle pressure?
There is a measure to cut the lines of laws under skin
Entering in through sand on the road.
There are cracks between footsteps and voices
Speaking in images cut off time and set loose in the fluid.

Day by day we are developed by whose hands?
By whose hands by whose hands.
There are choices.

Still Life X

No such thing as a still life
as life runs still flooding the till like pennies dropping off the new
york stock exchange,
like pennies rolling down spiral slides in the arcade fluorescence of
the price chopper lobby
on the whim of quarters wielding grinning helium witches on a
purple string.
We suck down H2 and cruise like the Hindenburg
while heads roll down marble escalators on Wall St.
and Rip Van Winkle never slept
Even while tears sleep on my cheeks like yellow dragons whispering
on clouds in the mountain.

No such thing as a still life
Only still living.

Apples and citrus blush in wood bowls under the kiss of
death on the tip of a paintbrush.
While globs of lipstick smear the canvas and back rooms
of brothels in the mirror lips smack candid suspended over velvet.
Like candy we suck out our juice while posies ring pink garland
string band waltzes around a garden of skulls in the sanguine moon.
Lace struts sultry on elephants marching in the salon and rings
hips rolling in the whorehouse river of buried aristocracies.

Honey drips and drops a fat beard in the tea glass while long beards
reel out on the silk pillows of bloodshot conversations,
Subtle intimations resonate in ears lined up at the cliff side,
fried off the rocking chair while stairs tumble down to the ocean.

And still
Life runs still hot through the still,
Steaming down muddy Kentucky rivers

fed by liquor and rage in the spring thaw,
While the winter of discontent flowers in the waning dusk
of Edison's child flickering static jump in the workshop.

Automatic flows the hand of speech
while automatic rifles slip out of assembly lines and we all say
AK is OK for me and shoot up kalashnikov concertos in brooklyn alleys.
While the human body lies still it's a battlefield for leeches,
Cruising on edward teach while the director strikes on waves
and weaves brass tapestries on Stravinsky's body.
Words blip like blots on the radar,
Drones fly liquid automation with *The Nation* spitting out of the
afterburners.
Insubordinate triggers flicker in the shrink's file and pile up shells
in jeep trunks while the dust bowl spreads faster than fungus in the west.
Van Gogh's grave is a detonation test while he rolls under modern dirt.
And life still rolls out never still in my kitchen as a melon sitting on a
vase slowly
turns black from one end spreading with white spots till it's hollow as
bones sucked dry.
I water it and it crumbles.

Film Noir Scene One

Darkness falls and blood smears the windows,
slowly puddling in alleys and
raining down into sewer tunnels,
as candles burn slightly in the reading room,
and the night rubs its oily muzzle on the window pane.

The ink jar on the desk is still warm,
filled with juice from the anus of
the squid lounging in his tank in the salon.
It is a great conversation piece
as cocktail glasses click around the table,
and beneath the window
a lead slug lays its deadly mucus
across the brains of a coka cola dealer,

And with a turgid snap,
his body lies
like a knocked up sweet sixteener
dreading the fury of family.
It lies on its back
on the cold bones of the pavement.
And blood mingles with blood leaking from the sky
as the earth's blood spills in the Gulf of Mexico
and the Persian Gulf,
and when the blood bank runs short
they pump me full of oil.

Shaded figures whisper in vaunted doorframes,
and flying buttresses wheel over
mice huddling in meadows.
The Earth is strapped down in the infirmary
getting the chemo of a dare.
No one waited for the knock from the stair.

We're all afraid of the elephant man
We're all afraid of the elephant man

And satellites wheel on warped wingspans
over deserts that crawl on their stomachs across Africa
America and Asia,
and Triple A offers high-quality roadside service
anywhere in the world.
Napoleon crawls on his stomach under the invalids
still dreaming of Siberia,
but an army never never crawls on its back like a crab,
even as its victims lie on their backs mouth gagged,
even when June falls under a cancerous sky.

Little crabs are crawling in the walls,
little crabs are crawling in the windy halls between bedsheets;
Venus is the brightest spot in the sky and she screams in the bed –
everyone loves a good quarantine when life is Hollywood.

The Bubonic Plague made a beautiful centerfold
in *National Geographic,*
and the candlelight rubs lightly the graphics of sex
between human adolescents
and oversized fluorescent beetles pulled from a popular manga series.
Conversation bubbles out of tippy bloody-marys
around the oak table
despite the greasy bartender's hands molesting the piano
keys in the corner
as f-sharps roll across the surface tension like kisses
off a cobra's tongue.
Professor Gill shouts "let me read you my poetry"
three times in birdsong
as the clock chimes one two eleven,

. . .

and the ball is still rolling in Prospero's abbey.
Nervous laughter reveals the fear that the slick street might slither in
through the window.

For the introverts there is a dream party in the bedroom
as all the guests lie asleep together on the bed,
calm as cubs in the den.
The wind rustles cracking dead branches high above the street and
ghosts whistle from the moon,
While a man and a woman
with shaved heads and hairy armpits rustle down
a downtrodden teenager
from a fistful of bills and cigarettes.
And deep in the Niger Delta, distinguished scientists
rustle down some stubborn
shelves of shale for a fistful of sweet crude ambrosia,
and we can drink a shot of kerosene while fasting for two days
to clear out our bodies of toxins.
The camera cuts to a runway where dazzling models
step one fish two fish
in elegant dresses forged of molten petroleum jelly
that we all lather over our bodies at the spa with slices of cucumbers,
aka rigid green hydrocarbon balloons.

And children scream soap me up sally
but we all gotta wait on the Brooklyn bridge
whether you're driving across
or driving off.

Trucks roll from Normandy to Naples to Normandy with potatoes.
The keen eye of the detective gazes to the stars
and notes satellites colliding and falling to earth,
undetectable to the remainder of the cast.
The ocean roars under shackles of garbage as life is no longer so
pacific as before.

Meanwhile,
the butler hides with a candlestick in the closet,
unseen.
End scene.

Design Stain

Silhouettes in short-sleeved stripes pace
In the wide sterile hall white in wall,
Texture blemished with scanty bumps in the plaster.
The sun already clasped its brass cover
Over the hands of time clicks muffled in the sky's pocket.
Time loses its witchy power in dimness,
Power stitched into light.

A cool violet settles and clings to
Vast panes of glass not yet stained.
Shadows inch their spears into the wide
Offices of Bertrand, Blais & Gaudette,
Drawn figures move slow and graceful,
Almost real humans.
Kinesis stokes the mind's appetite
Before pens swoop predatorial to
Landscapes of paper prone on the table.
Tiny glints in the carpeting shade,
Eyes are the only sources of light –
Glances develop subtle motions
To render the world a zoo.
Pencil lines are all it takes
For the plaster to set
Under the cool leadership of Gaudette.
Imagine that we are mannequins.
The scene is much like a cartoon

But soon, the razor lines of shadow
Shift. The figures lean in a prism,
Dripping sweat in silky cotton.
There is no more light –
Only gradients of gray.
Industrial design may be sexual.

The only music is industrial.
Papers crinkling and scuffing on the table
While figures shift stop-motion.
A gray back thumps on the workspace.
Papers leap like scared pigeons, like millions.
It is a silent movie, set to imagined music.
Electronic montage of urban sounds
Yet all the same, cloistered. Inward,
Even while sexy. Pencil scratches give way
To fingernails. Moans run hollow from throat
To throat without bodies and skin.
The graphite soaked plans animating
Concrete walls to ring the animal tents often
Referred to as 'residential zones'
Begin to soak in genital fluids,
Grainy, sketched with the side of a pencil.
Gaudette may be upset.
Table legs tremble, slowly at first.
Legs are full of nerves, and conduct tension.
Hatch-marking pencils get frantic.
Plans chart lines on tables and constellations
Often stained by the liquid impulses
Of human desires –
Not to say that we are liars.

Indigo Symphony

Indigo is my fury as we flush like five hearts across the whammy bar
landscape of all night old time dance parties in long johns and silver
pickups whining long sustains as we pick each other up and pick up
where we left off in lost memories of love
Cruising the faltering main street in a beat up pickup with neon
hecklers swinging from a single hinge
swinging from the memory of the dodo bird
You stick your neck out like an ostrich you're gonna hang
But we can flood heads down obscure in the executioners' hood as a
scaffold sings operas in the Wall St. fluorescence we'll blow up like a
coal impoundment strapped with dynamite as strapping young
hillbillies drive forklifts in the generating station
Roads wind like rattlers through the shifting hillsides
of the chain's interior

Massey Energy is a suicide bomber across the bedridden fever
dreams of West Virginia
There is a terrorist in the White House still surprising after forty
three other times?
Spacebag red wine is nothing but white wine mixed with blood from
the blood bank and queers are public enemy number one when the
public bloodstream is ill
Criminality is contagious as the Hudson Valley explodes silent in the
memory of derelict family mafias buck teeth sing doe re mi in the
back of pine-covered hills
Smoky the Bear is an arson and London Bridge is falling shantih
shantih shantih as Somali Pirates sing proud shanties over the
monsoon season tears flowing from toxic barrels dumped in the
Indian Ocean beyond the Italian backyard backwater
The Barbary Coast whistles assassin heresies in solidarity from the
wide eyes of fallen pirates on the ocean floor
lungs pull deep breath under the crushing brine of years

Bananas and Bananas and Bananas and thick dockyard cocks lying
like copperheads in the year-round sunset
crested dusk of yellow fever dictatorships
Bananas hitch a ride on great galleons as white pine mast forests are
stolen by white hands in the albino terror midnight of the
Massachusetts grave coast
How can an ocean hold so many secrets
without seeing a psychologist?
There's a ring around the pink posies as lips smack in anticipation
There's a ring around the moon so huge and golden I've never seen
as we skate on the ice frozen gleaming
so white it's almost green in midstream
frozen in horizontal waterfalls with piled icicles of racing velocity as
if it was all instantaneous
It all happens so fast a month later after a bender this kid walks
downstream on the same St. Francis when vodka burning in the lungs
vaporizing the dry frosty air
The ice opens in the crack of snare silent and water erupts still in the
silent spring of a second
Holes open and close when they want to – he was a father – we all speak
when we want to and voter ballots flood the solid waste management
system on the seventh of November
love burns on in the shell of an ember.

Indigo is my fury as we rush like samurai born again as beatniks
across the mechanized
Workhouse Graveyard Strip Mall Landscape of choose your own
Psychiatric Disorder Novels
We all want a pill – we all wanna chill out at the doctor's office while
trust was long ago buried in the bottom
of an empty Valium bottle and chucked

. . .

Epiphanies glare out the windows of second floor yoga studios and
strip clubs and hare krishna hare krishna hare hare hare and karaoke
night at the bar with underground
German metal classics churches have fled churches and hidden in the
circuitry of TVs in bowling alleys and porno web sites and Japanese
Blow-up Life-time Sex Partner Dolls
and the Self-Help section at Barnes & Noble and plummeting at
terminal velocity through the gasping air over Broadway—the game
ain't over. We are not just old dried dog shits by the sidewalk next to
half-eaten pizza crusts.

Gods are born in the fluid circuitry of the earth machine as we are all
sacred creatures
Divinity may flow with the accuracy of assassination into the
interface of the free world and the free world may crumble
percussive in geologic harmonies as it collapses under the weight of
its own irony we can kill dictators with the four elements
The banjo rips a red solo in the shimmering dark as we're all drunk in
the glow of our own spirits love flows from the dregs and summons
itself in smoke rising like the words of an underworld banshee
revealing itself in a cave.

Indigo is my fury as love pools all night between the bedsheets and
we rise with the sun to burn the hell out of this world
Biting skin as teeth gather and clack like bullets rubbing shells on the
ammo belt
And we know what we felt
There is nothing here to stop us
but ourselves.

Écorcher la Nuit

The sterling intensity of this swollen night opens out like a flower
Beckoning, thrusting into the first falling spears of the morning light
Opens like a star bursting in joyous agony in the eternal song of
The flame churning inside its gut
And coming
And coming
Forever
Through our ears and nose and eyes and throats
The luminosity of a million suns
Dancing a twisted tango
Burning out in little lanterns over the charred blanket
of a summer's night
A winter's night
Snowflakes turning pirouettes on the silent wind
Glistening in icy reflection of the horrid fires above
Snow falling like a shower of broken glass over the crude body
of an asphalt cookie sheet
Bouncing and tinkling o'er the ground like raindrops and marbles
And prickling down into the impermeable black membrane of hell
Some sickly Heidegger swimming in the ocean ooze of being
Where life may refuse to be stamped out by the shuddering folds of dark
Thick in the sweat of a dream of a river
Flowing between bodies
Little geysers sending drops and showers
And thirsty pores sucking down their fill
Licking saline streams and hard nipples beckoning in the never
A shooting star may sit a million years in *nulle part*
Just to swim a catapult stream arcing a lover's back across the sky
A fire born for one beaming moment
One movement
For those who dare swipe at the jaws of the heavens

. . .

And cackle the grinning maw of a skeleton
To know that one who lives in death
Is a flower
Roots crackling whips on wind electric
The lightning flare of suckling fibers twisting a faint medusa
Revel in the wanting darkness grotesque
Over the sunken ashes of a house of mirrors
The real horror
To those who have learned to fear
Is the bathhouse of terrors
Swimming in steamy saunas and sultry waters
With snakes and feathers, fucked up grins and leather
Smacking the bars on a cage of desire
Plunging in pools of moonlight and stretching limbs in the velvet
To walk fearless in the midnight of good and evil
Stars fires limbs lovers tired sins
Burning on the whim of a drunken flower
Swollen to burst on the mead of a loving nothing
All the living love forgotten splayed out like crickets on the watch
table of science
But the sitting stars curled up in excess of sweating honey glands
Timed to explode in a shower of nectar and blood
On the phoenix altar
Set upon by the morning's first spears of light
Skulls grinning a life given freely to a new day
Wings of pollen pirouetting like yellow snowflakes
Catching and magnifying each twist of light
See-sawing on the silent wind
And dropping one by one
Ever so slowly
On a day that is
    Coming
    Coming
    Forever

Carnival of Words '11

For souls it is death to become water, for water it is death to become earth; out of earth water arises, out of water soul.

Heraclitus

I — *For Every Action*

What if words could destroy it all?
Carefully placed adjectives clogging pipes
Frozen to burst mudded up to burst,
Drowning in run-on description and pocked up like a
Pick cushion impaled by precision pins sticking out of cheeks,
Verbs wired to kitchen timers
Cached in corners of ministry offices
Waiting for their time to come.

Who isn't waiting for the time to come?
Who isn't waiting outside some thick metal door,
Lying face down on the floor in the swelling heat of August,
Lying down because some lieutenant told you to
Because he told you he loved you.
What if words could pick you back up on your feet
And spit out of your mouth with loose teeth
Dangling from years of whiskey.

And you could wrap your hands up in adverbs,
Efficiently kicking the lieutenant's ass —
Little monosyllabic nouns dripping into the oil pan
Of the secret service fleet of suburbans,
Until they start their engines.
Gentlemen: explode
Motors flip over diving boards of heat,
Without lubrication
They crunch.
And words spit sinister out of the exhaust pipe,
Sputtering one last stanza
Before suicide.

And they all fall down.
One by one they all fall downsizing their own calling

To the security of the state.
Phones ringing coded statements,
Interjections cutting razor lines across
Apocryphal headlines.
The media is confused
Because they don't have words.
They only have typeset printed into the protocol
Of 3-gig processors that at the end of the day
Don't really know anything –
They just process.

And the crisis idles on motionless
With a fog impeding its own comprehension.
And when there's no words to tell you how to panic,
Do you panic harder or softer?
And does it really matter if you're watching hardcore porn or softcore?
When sadofreaks in gas masks burst in your bedroom door
And say, we're with Interpol.
And you say I'm from the other pole of the earth.
And the lightning rod of the spectrum conducts political
Electricity through ear to ear inconsistencies.
The spectrum of light splits suicidal in the fixture
And words fixed in the set of your mind spill
Out on the stoop out on the street
Sliding across the slick lips of the pigs in the doorframe. Just say:

I have words to slip out of your handcuffs.
I have words to slide your skin out of blue canvas.
And they spill out line after line
Like strokes of the brush on the green canvas army tent
Undone. Seams separated,
Strung up on the wall.
The view of my eyes is personal.
Do not hang me in a museum,
Do not string my words up on billboards –

. . .

Unless they spray out so heavy the billboard drops,
Fast as five tons of metal,
To the roiling mob of King St. West rush hour.
Rubber tires running to the west,
Never forgetting forty-niners
While rolling advertisements stampede in reverse –
In contrast to a culture that flows in one direction,
Depending on the time of day.
We call it mobile marketing.
Deleuze and Guattari call it
The Nomadic War Machine.
Word machine—warding against herding fascist rhetoric,
Gathering on helpless blades of grass in city parks,
While few witness their congregations at dawn.
No one sees it coming.
There is nothing more nomadic than a word.
A word can circumnavigate the globe five times in a day –
It can send out microalphabetical research squads in the solar system.
Light is a word
And it gave birth to the world.
While the crude lips of politicians
[In the modern mediatic sense]
Like to swallow fire and put out lights in the
Incoming tide of dusky –
Bedtime, kids. And tuck us in on the cutting edge
Of a curfew. Go to sleep little baby.
There's nothing wrong. You can sleep all day
Staring at spreadsheets. Conference calls clinging
To pastoral passé before eyes shot Facebook comments
Silent. They tell us to sleep tight—and they'll sleep
When they're dead. In the city that never sleeps,
All we can do is make sure
They keep their promise
Sooner than they planned.

II – *An Equal and Opposite Reaction*

Real eyes scan the dictionary pages,
Seeking definitions to problems rolling out of
Bar graphs, line charts—beating hearts
Bar the participation of emotions,
In a system that destroys human motion
Under the treads of a tank that has never stopped
Since 1916.

Skid marks criss-cross my face
Since the day I was born.
Steel helmets crush the meaning of words
That once lay calm under my scalp.
They will never come out again.
How many will never come out again
From where they are hiding?
In bunkers and tunnels,
In bedrooms pasted up with memories of childhood.
With old faces twisted in new skins every day,
Never getting older –
Only turning into devious betrayals
Of what the good guys once meant to us.

How can aging joys and heroes say anything
While bombs explode on the street outside?
How can politicians cease to be robots
Until they strip the face off their skins,
Expose the wires lining steel-enforced skulls?
Craning to exude humanity,
Straining to bury the vestiges of doubt
Lying steady in trenches long forgotten—Except by words.

But my skin is no strip mine
For new laws to extract the essence of

. . .

A time that refuses to dilute its fervor
Into a tincture –
So long as words pile up on callused fingertips,
As long as pens pile up in mass graves,
And intelligence forsakes the memory of
A single word: responsibility.

Day by day,
In classrooms besieged by deadly
AV programming—scanning the perky rabbit,
Ears wrapped in propaganda, for young audiences –
I will never submit
To brain scans rub-on sun tans,
Rub on foreplay with the seductive power
Of legislation.
Masturbation expands in the realm of forgetfulness,
But I will never forget to speak,
And smuggle bullets in my cheeks
Until there is nothing left
But to shoot old yellow teeth out of a slingshot.
They all fall out –
They all fall down.

I'll be ready as a Freddy with a chainsaw,
Words hanging on the old brass balance of the law –
Ready to fall off the desk and crack on the floor.
Chains are fragile,
And lined bureaucratic hands have trouble measuring mass.
The chain that steadies the balance
May soon measure itself around powdered necks,
Wound up gleeful as a jack-in-the-box
On Christmas morning.

Nuclear winter is white—even in California.
Little smiles gather around yellowing trees
And the emphatic radio warnings to STAY HOME –
Until you watch words
Snowing from the skyscrapers, from the thick clouds,
From the gathering mass of an earthly fervor to live,
Blanketing old statues of massacre heroes,
Melting on the wide-open eyes of industrialists,
Burning like witches in water,
And piling up wisdom
Thick enough to walk in it,
Make balls and throw it,
Boil it and drink it,
And finally sleep with the calming cold:

To know that even if the world lies aching
Bleeding screaming raped behind a dumpster,
It can live on
If the rapist is dead.

III – *Corn Starch*

Words gather like phlegm in the back of my throat
in the fount of my lungs
And I cough and spray yellow spittle on the carcinogenic
dust of the sidewalk,
So white and clean—the smooth baby's ass of California beaches
Spread with a butter knife across bourgeois pedestrian walkways
Slowly encircling the world. But it is only one world inside many.
Time to dam a river and call it the Lake of Nations.
Damnation rings hollow in ears sporting digital headphones,
running in nike
Around a lake born of narcissism mixed with concrete.
Thick walls impede the motion of poets spawning in September.
The psyche subjects itself to self-examination stretching nylon shorts –
Well-to-do young families stray fearful at the scent of fools in
Old flannel spitting tobacco and disease in the public park.
Saliva carries venomous connotations in a language that dubs
The human body a sealed container, the passage of liquids
Only permitted in designated zones.
Women don't bleed anymore they only glisten,
Diluting crimson with the clarity of methamphetamines.
Perhaps freaks drink menstrual blood in pagan rituals,
But only in the imagination of horror tycoons.
These are only words.
Nothing can be trusted until you see it
Climbing through the plasma screen
In real-time live broadcast of the highest quality,
Life-size digitized limbs stretch out in your living room
And strangle you to death—satiated in a subdue
Sadomasochist entertainment media,
On your new leather couch from Ikea.

Words coagulate thick as thieves
And congest the esophagus of society as carbon monoxide pumps
Out of thick four-lane boulevards choking in clouds of humidity.
The sun may be hot but the burning smoke cools our flesh,
Cells blinded by the acid stench of fresh tar infusing in long days.
Tongues dangle inarticulate,
And we drip unformed syllables on our own shoes.
Step by step we revert to the anal stage,
Retention suits holding our flaccid humanity in privatized sacks
Of organs. Schmoozing prostitutes liquored up in the Harvard
MBA job fair, dry tongues licking cheese cubes on toothpicks –
Higher education evaporates bodily fluids.
Instincts once sharp loll vapid in uniform temperatures,
Uniform dress code and uniform Slap Your Ass
In Front Of A Computer,
Unable to compute that climate control,
like any mechanical construct,
Is a lie. Even if it works in offices
It cannot work in the world.

And once-human bodies dry up like old words
Rotting in the ashes of Alexandria.
What happens to a letter when it decomposes?
Phonetics are slow to decay in dry throats.
Hard to relax as slowly crisping eyes tear up, reflexes
Paralyzed in desert heat witnessing the slow decay of a body stretching
Out from your vision,
While flies feast on disappointment, landing on crusty tongues.
The only thing left to say cracks in the voice box,
Prone and defenseless,
Where monsoon-thirsty ground splits under the sunfire,
And soon there is nothing left to say
But what can be said on the epitaph

. . .

Of an oasis of living potential,
Petrified speechless in a surrealist's nightmare photograph,
Seasoned with words—good only to burn.
Useless in the Mojave Spitfire,
Cracked lips can starve
Sucking on the exhaust pipe.
Civilization leaves nothing untouched.

IV – *Kevorkian Jeopardy*

Waiting for the prognosis –
On chairs of chipboard pressed from old bones,
Bodies donated to science.
Alliances are drawn on shabby pieces of paper pressed against
bathroom walls.
Statesmen could divide the world on a cocaine binge
For the love of efficiency.
Speed is the new gospel,
Except for those tied to chipboard chairs in the waiting room,
Waiting for a truck stacked high with news magazines from 2003.
The patients could mummify themselves in papier maché,
While waiting for the doctor to call,
Or the voice to speak from high above—Pick a Number.
Deep in slumber it is impossible.
Bathing in harsh ceiling lamps glade plug-ins
No more need for perfume.
Just spray the whole room,
Spray the whole restaurant –
Everyone can vote on a flavor.
Or get rubbed down by a dictator
Stalking in the shadows behind the dishwasher,
Plotting the coup d'état of Table Five.
You could fuck on the plate of brownies à la mode.
Nobody minds as long as there's no blood.
As long as your semen is perfect pH 7,
As long as zeroes chase the decimal point to infinity,
As long as your pants conform to regional dress by-laws A5-A17.
Might as well keep on waiting,
Filling up canopic jars behind the kids' toy corner,
Playing Beethoven on the attention bell,
Stringing velvet treehouses over the attention span.
Walls papered with spandex keep us safe.
Lung juice pumps out of stainless vents devoid of voices.

. . .

Running in place is a good pastime
Until one goes for an illicit look into the doctor's office.
The investigation reveals
The MD lying face down in a puddle of words,
Spilled from the pharmaceutical briefcase of Pfizer reps.
We leave our own words on his back,
Before we walk out.

V — *Urban Renewal*

There is a certain syntax of strategy
Seeping through the surrounding architecture,
Bleeding brightly tattooed color-lines in blue prints,
Shifting restless on the drafting table.
Labels stick, glued to their own desires.
Hierarchies of needs programmed into the angle of
Effluent pipes pumping into the toilets' discharge.
Words can only be stacked so deep into the sky
Before they crumble,
Scratching guttural in the streaks of dirt lined with broken glass
At the side of the road.
One by one waiting for their turn
To drop into the sewer.
Words drop out of my eyes and trip me underfoot
As I stagger through the grid-like grammar of the city.
You can try to teach me but full sentences
Lack the properties to stick.
They like to lick their own pride
And fill up lawbooks accumulating from the Enlightenment,
Streets writing over forgotten makeshift
graves in poor neighborhoods.
Old shacks lying in the mud of languages that long ago
Flew the coop, fled with chickens
seeking liberty—trapped in factories.
Secret histories buried in the argon shrieks of shopping centers
Metropolitan stripping out in straight lines,
According to lazy eyes. Stick to the road:
The straight path runs the yard-stick of second-grade grammar.
Tired legs stick to a path ingrained and forgotten.
Grains forget the magic words breathed to give them life,
Rewritten in bastard tongues of numbers and letters,
Screwed into the ink of double helix papers,

. . .

Downloaded into the memory of cellulose.
Rejection is not an option –
We have to feed seven billion
With paper signs advertising Cargill fertilizers,
With tractors sucked dry from the bowels of mountains,
Lubricated in dehydrating oils.
Steel throats spouting smoke syllables –
And we choke even in the country.
Old mills press their machines into the dirt,
While human desires flock to pulping grounds
On the mean streets of financial capitals.
Old rascals flip houses like spitting out kick flips on picnic benches –
Without a word.
Legs spread out deep tarred in the erasure of old farms.
Lie down on their backs, forfeit the will to walk,
While one little piggy wiggles to say:
Take me to the market.
Take me to the slaughterhouse.
String me up with the cattle –
I'll remember the drill that goes into the brain.
Take me to the school and we will sit.
The ashes will teach me.
Words buried in thick textbooks,
Without the dignity of a funeral.
Take me to where my mother reads to me –
Take me to where the fire read to me,
Ancient verse spoken into sparks.
The coals hold the memory of the world,
And the old ways written into song
Long-forgotten in new blueprints spinning off xeroxes,
Painted over and over on the stomping grounds of cities.
Words that were lost can be found

When we lose ourselves in the forest.
Springs gurgle rimeless philosophies,
Leaves bristle on branches ready to talk,
But not to lie on the talking couch.
We can speak when we drink the waters running
Down from the mountaintops.
We can talk silent, grinding out old habits
Of forgetting with words.
Lips see no need to flap, whining like gulls.
Who learn words without the syntax of fear?
Cruising sweet in the clearing –
The stars will guide us.
But where we end up
Will not be where we started,
And when we die,
Lips dry dry in the desert,
We will be smiling.

VI — *Tactics*

The art of war
Once written in words
Blasphemed in the burning code of digits.
Drones singing inhuman synthesizers in dry airs,
Hawks sing their own praises in five-sided compounds.
Robotic eyes glaring down from space
May gleam in their own souls
When mirrors come down from the hills on horseback,
Fires blazing out of the four branches' sockets,
And simple words spoken slow and long
May scratch out hidden meanings in the shadows,
Reviving arts long forgotten still unseen. Striking surprise,
Gong claps on the side of the head and officers fall dizzy.
The art may be cursed but it is not forgotten.

It may return on the wings of words,
Pigeons flooding windows bearing scrolls
Seeing out of skulls still afloat from the Civil War.
Extinction is no excuse
To go on erecting machines.
Time is no excuse to keep riding electric sidewalks.
There is no use to forget words,
Vengeful as old bones
Popping out of death,
Eyes scanty snaking out of skulls
To bring facts on a phoenix drop,
Descending from warriors
That may die in skin,
But live on in words.

VII — *El Chupacabra*

Words Words Words Words Words
Constructed on Etch-A-Sketch rhythms.
Standing up Frankenstein-Style in graphite shavings –
Shave our legs and grind down the hairs to a powder.
It is a tool for language.
Erector set stand-up steel-frame scaffold, words rise
From the ground steaming, nailed-together makeshift structures,
One by one the pieces fit together.
It lives it lives screams the mad doctor glasses falling down his nose,
Forethought falling by the wayside. Words kill instincts –
Sharp as a bullet tight as a target,
Singing lyric poetry in the rifle range.
We have to test our abilities before we can strike down Goliath.
Humanoid in appearance but he is a machine
And he can be shut down. Tie down his legs
Like star wars chicken-walkers tripping,
Or climb inside the heart find the control room we all have it.
Hack the mainframe he may be fierce but he is tame.
No sequence of numbers can encrypt the ferocity
of strong wills branded,
Hot on drunk skin evaporating inhibitions
in the dim light of struggle.
Machines only bleed electric coals, kissing sparks in the firelight,
Oil running like water through mechanical muscles.
Keep the dead alive in robot form metal legs strutting.
Hubris crunches in the electromagnetic storm.
Old Testament stories pickled in code can still be killed
When they walk. Volcanic eyes menace our free motion.
Monsters are built into operating protocols,
Engineering norms volley arrows into the heart of the natural
Saturated in artificial flavors in fat bulked up from corn on steroids.

. . .

Stereotypical lines draw up the square frame of bionic manipulation,
Stipulating the run sequence.
Run-down steps collapse in the basement;
Try to forget the furnace that burns, yellow eyes
Jack-O'-Lanterns coming to life in metal rattles at midnight,
Pumping hot water hot air energizing meaningless conversations.
The self-destruct sequence sits idle in old lettering systems.
We just punch it in
And punch in the face of Frankenstein.

VIII — *Lunatic Etymology*

Words return eternal when the mind slows.
Eyes roll back as the tide recedes and the moon drops quiet
Over dark hillsides retreating from another night.
Eyesight kills the warm fire of voices
Evergreen frozen shimmering bright across the foreground.
To see is cold—summoning space and distance.
Separation sits, cool evidence lined up on the bookshelf.
Desk sitting empty waiting for inspiration,
The Oxford is a taxonomy of alienation.
Art smirks hanging on resentful nails.
They whisper: take me out of here when the lights are gone.
They long for skin or magma bleeding hot in the Earth's heart.
Tectonic veins wrap us all in double-helix body bags,
So we can talk but no longer see,
Telling stories into the fire
Where I am the ghost,
And the host of the party is lost in thought.
For eons we sought to smuggle illegal words in body cavities.
So many today would like to just float calm, eyes open
To see—and drown.

The sound of eyes rolling deep into the skull –
Deep sea exploration in the human body,
Retina sliding casual down my gullet.
Swallow sight with bird song returning in the spring.
The tide will always come back,
Whether we come with it
Or stay with the salt.

IX – *Lupercalia / Compendia*

Old words shove their alphabets down once-resistant throats
Lined up for a mug shot –
Stretched-up posture for posterity in the annals of the legal system,
Barbaric codes jotted down in vellum-bound volumes
Archived in the catacombs,
While the bones of cryptic edicts
Assemble in the sepulcher of hard drives gathering dust.
The Holy Roman Empire stretches bony fingers across
Pages that live on unburied corpses
Exposing themselves on the linoleum floor
Of society—flayed by the sunlight picked on by birds.
An assassin can split throats with a paper cut,
Turn coats with the twist of a spoken finger,
Open locks with a cursed breath of smoke.
The timbre of deadly voices echoes across the panic space
Of silent bedrooms beating ever faster
In the night's climax. Eyes flutter rapid,
Wings flap terror in the cage.
So many solemn feet clog through the day,
Never knowing who is master of the air encoded around them.
Cold eyes fail to see that the air is alive,
Blood coarsing rampant through the oxygen,
Thinned to near-starvation in the mounting quiet.
Music thumping in every fat window lined with skinny fashion,
Synthetic limbs carrying self-conscious cash pockets into the store
While rockets blast off blind pride into the stars.

One-day words run through the mind
On four-track tape spinning on reels of gray matter,
Fused into stainless.
Eyes glaze into mirror screens.
Blinking is free energy to pump the cassette deck.

The needle turns out spiraling shots of vinyl blood,
Injecting arteries from the inside.
Like that we keep walking,
Lurching step by step into the future.
At school pupils sit down dilating swollen limbs and rest,
While pedagogy technicians plug informatics into the direct current.
USB in straight under the earlobe.
All We Need To Know at the speed of light.
Speed-dating surpassing comets,
Direct network connections revealing personal
Traits converted to ones and zeroes.
This is how education can save the nuclear family.
Nuclear plastic running coils deep into the brain
Grabs the human past by the throat.
Copper retinas gaze into bony eyes dredged out by worms.
The tape begins to scratch and gristle at the end.
The hunger for old words begins to gnaw in the throat
While modern eyes cloud up with snow.

———————————

X — *Amor Fati*

Deception cracks the bell of fate,
Splitting blood cells like atoms.
Civil war turns red in the blood stream.
Bullets crack in mid-atmospheric flight.
Eyes are rent down the middle in divergence.
Scalp rumbles, mimics the belching of the earth
While pupils tend to quake in their wooden chairs,
Mathematics pressing groaning lights straight into both eyes.
Walk home half blinded without words.
Nobody heard the fear present in optometry –
Easy to lose track of what the heart pumps through the body.
Knowledge may be wordless but there is music if we listen.
Cut the magnetic tape tying down dizzy heads,
Encoded with lies that hide in books.
Nothing left but to look at stricken faces strangled in smiles,
Rubbing cheeks blushing with wine,
Feasting on sacrificial brains in the punch bowl.
The party goes late but some are sleeping.
Contrary to the marketing of snacks,
The party mix is a chemical cocktail that blinds us to fate.
And while you roll into bed blacked out remember:
Words may not come back the way you expect,
But they always come back.

Words Words Words Words
Hidden in the liberty bell—gave it its crack.
One day it will rend itself in two beautiful iron bowls,
Falling to the brick below.
Tongue and eyes battle each other,
Relentless as the west wind.
Manifest Destiny turns its hungry gaze to the inside
And turns kamikaze.

Words come to life in ancient symbols and gestures to call the rain,
To call the fury of gales shrieking banshees floating.
The sky is fearsome because it is unknown.
Clouds saturate with water and anger.
Wool slowly deteriorates in puddles and falls off eyeballs.
Clarity comes with the setting of the sun.
Memories refract off the whites sailing quick from before history,
We sing to remember—gathered in the fire,
coals carrying heat from old blood.
Soaked fabric cools the skin. Shiver and quake,
We gasp coming up from the ocean.
Salty are the words that dry skin puckers and smiles suck into bones.
Reanimation requires faith
And the sun carries fate blazing across the universe,
So Goliath cannot stand
Under the pressure of a word.

XI – *Lucky Number 13*

Twisting the home of luck in blind action,
The hand grips the knife handle firm.
Handlebars drop fast as the face to the curb –
Sometimes pain comes with glee.
The hill carries fire down to the valley,
Spirits running wild in exhaustion.
Pictures cycle pre-linguistic
In an ocular landscape oscillating readiness.
Lips are the arteries of communication.
Luck flows through mycelia,
Pops up happy little heads from the damp floor.
Needles gather in vacant lots and pine forests.
Strung out agony resonates in the poetic eye,
Looking blind in the back hands searching ever forward,
Marching through the cave seeing by stalactites.
Words crouch like bats sleeping on the ceiling,
Chasing rodents and seeking cacophony in the hot dark,
No longer seeing no longer speaking.
There is a joy in silence.
Sleep carries slowing thoughts walking steady in the forest,
Feet mingle with decay.
Fungal infection may turn us monsters,
Seeking the company of satyrs.
Give me horns and I will blow a flute.
Give me hooves and I will sing.
Give me a ring in my nose
And I will stampede through the dusty streets,
Tumbleweeds running my electoral campaign,
Sacrificing china shops for fertility and eating on the floor –
Goring the ego a hundred times over.
Matadors compressing into old black and white photographs.
There is no luck left in the World Trade Centers.

While the very word may tumble limp,
Unglued from the NASDAQ
Daily scroll reeling out regrets,
The moon may carry new fortunes in its bloody rising
So huge, hanging on the horizon.
While the lucky thirteen turn-around warriors
Gather on the edge of trees pot-latches whining pressure release tones
Revel in the warmth of possessions feeding the fire.
We can burn it all
But keep our words.

www.ingramcontent.com/pod-product-compliance
Lightning Source LLC
LaVergne TN
LVHW041236080426
835508LV00011B/1238